Simple Thoughts That Can Change Your Life

Gerald G. Jampolsky, M.D.
& Diane V. Cirincione, Ph.D.

CELESTIALARTS
Berkeley • Toronto

CELESTIALARTS

PO Box 7123
Berkeley, California 94707
www.tenspeed.com

Celestial Arts books are distributed in Canada by Ten Speed Canada, in the United Kingdom and Europe by Airlift Books, in Australia by Simon & Schuster Australia, in New Zealand by Southern Publishers Group, in South Africa by Real Books, and in Singapore, Malaysia, Hong Kong, and Thailand by Berkeley Books.

Cover and text design by Greene Design

Library of Congress Cataloging-in-Publication Data on file with the publisher

Printed in Canada

1 2 3 4 5 6 - 06 05 04 03 02 01

Dedication

This book is dedicated to our dear friends, Hal and Dorothy Thau, whose friendship, constant love, encouragement, and support continue to be a major blessing in our lives.

Preface

Many of our parents told us when we were children not to put too much food in our mouths and to eat one bite at a time.

The same thing may be true for what we put in our minds. This book is filled with simple thoughts—one sentence in length. We recommend that you take one thought at a time.

Like food, it may be good to take time to chew on each thought slowly, taste it, and give yourself time to savor them. If the thought doesn't seem palatable, you don't have to swallow it. You may, however, want to come back to that thought at another time, with a new look, and reexamine it to see if it might now be more to your liking.

May you have a good appetite and happy reading.

Introduction

Our thoughts and beliefs are powerful determinants of the course of our lives. They determine what we see and what we experience, and they create our reality. Our thoughts are not just concepts, but there is an energy within our words that affects us and the world that we think we see. Perhaps the greatest gift that has been given to humankind is the power to determine what thoughts we put into our minds.

We have the power to choose negative, toxic, self-destructive, and judgmental thoughts that bring about conflict and separation, or we can choose thoughts that are positive, creative, loving, giving, and forgiving, and ones that can bring about joining, peace, and joy. Each day we can choose to awaken with just one single goal, peace of mind, and to remind ourselves that our peace of mind will depend on the thoughts we choose to put in our minds and not on the circumstances of our lives.

Many of the concepts in this book have an underlying premise based on "Attitudinal Healing," the core foundation of our work over the last twenty-five years. Attitudinal Healing is based on the belief that it is not people or conditions outside of ourselves that cause us distress, but that, ultimately, it is our own thoughts and attitudes that cause us to be upset. It defines "health as inner peace" and "healing as the letting go of fear."

Books and tapes exploring Attitudinal Healing in more depth are listed in the back of the book.

Suggestions for digesting "Simple Thoughts" so they can change your life include:

1. When you wake up in the morning, lie in bed for a few minutes and give thanks for the blessings you have in your life, choosing to think of only positive things.

2. Resist the temptation to think about your "to do" list.

3. Do your best to still your mind by imagining that there is a powerful light beam inside of you. Begin to shine your light on the people you love and the people you know who are fearful and suffering from lack of love.

4. While still in bed, read what the thought for the day is. Read it slowly and let it just rest there softly in your heart and in your mind. Now imagine that this thought is being carried by your blood vessels to every cell in your body, so that the thought is becoming at one with the very essence of your being.

5. Before breakfast, be willing to take time to write the

thought of the day on a piece of paper or a 3 x 5-inch card that you can keep with you for the rest of the day.

6. Be willing to sit down for just five minutes. Read the thought slowly and then close your eyes and immerse yourself in the thought.

7. Motivate yourself to read the thought of the day as often as possible throughout the day and allow the thought to trickle in and out of consciousness.

8. Strive for simplicity and balance as you go through the day.

9. Gently remind yourself that your thoughts not only affect your health and the world that you see, but also everything else in your life.

10. It makes little difference whether you begin this book in the middle, at the beginning, or starting with the end. We do suggest, however, that you read the Epilogue on page 113 first and reread it every evening for a week or more just before retiring for bed.

It is my logical,
rational mind
that
puts limits
on
what is possible.

Relief from all stress
comes from healing
the attitudes
in the mind.

*If only we would learn
to have the courage
to experience the pain
of our
unexpressed grief.*

*Freedom occurs
the moment
I let go
of my attachments.*

*True healing
has more to do
with listening and
unconditional love
than with trying to
fix people up.*

*I can choose
peace of mind
as my only goal
each and
every day.*

A friend is someone
who has seen you
at your worst
and still loves you.

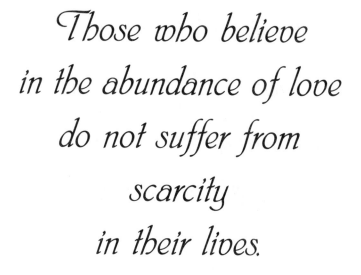

Those who believe
in the abundance of love
do not suffer from
scarcity
in their lives.

*Our greatest
underlying fears
are our fear of death,
abandonment
and
separation.*

*Others
don't have to change
in order for me
to be
happy.*

*Today
I will see no value
in comparing myself
with others.*

It is, ultimately, never anything else but our own thoughts that hurt us.

Possessiveness
is of the ego,
which is limitless
in its desire to
control people and
own things.

*Healing
begins the moment
we stop
judging.*

*If I am
a reflection of nature,
then it is the
only mirror I want.*

*Perhaps
the most important
equation in the world
is that the fullness of
one's heart
is directly proportional
to how much
love one gives.*

Peace will elude me
as long as I believe
that anger
brings me something
I really want.

*Butterflies teach us
that
embracing change
promises
transformation and
freedom.*

*Serenity
and tranquillity
are experienced
when we decide
to make
going inside of our
hearts a priority.*

Forgiveness
is the greatest
healer
of all.

Today I will accept responsibility for my own happiness.

The secret to
being happy
is to give up
all
of my judgments.

Staying in the present
prevents my getting
stuck
in the fear
of the past
or future.

I may not be able
to control
the outside world,
but I can control
the thoughts
in my
own mind.

Inner peace comes
when I no longer
choose
to see the shadows
in anyone's past,
including
my own.

Lies are like tails,
because
they always follow
you.

The quality of my life
will be determined
by how much
I give
to others.

I will see no value
in hurting others
or myself
with either my
thoughts, words,
or deeds.

*When loving, caring
and hugging
become as essential
as eating,
perhaps many of the
illnesses known to
humankind
will disappear.*

If you want to get where you want to go, you first have to leave where you are.

*Letting go
and letting God
are one and
the same.*

Forgiving others
and myself totally
with no exceptions
is
the key to
inner peace,
happiness, and freedom.

Live each day
as if
there is no enemy
and
there is no one
to blame.

*Let me remember
that stillness
is as essential to the
soul
as food is to
the body.*

Much of the pain
we suffer in life
is caused by our
beliefs
that our self-made
illusions
are real.

*The world would
become a better place
if
how much I love
became
more important than
how much I achieve.*

When we are

at

a loss for words

is when

we often hear

our answers.

*Home
is not where
your hat is, but
where
your heart is.*

You have 20/20
spiritual vision
when a weed
looks
as magnificent to you
as
a beautiful flower.

When you know that
children's chatter
is
a blessing,
the chatter
no longer sounds
like noise.

Following your heart

means

not making your

intellect

your

God.

Self-forgetfulness

is

a way

to

unconditional love.

We imprison ourselves
in darkness
because of guilt
and
attack thoughts
we
still hold on to.

Would not the world
be
different if each
of us
lived a life
for giving
and forgiving?

If you knew that
this
would be your last day
on earth,
wouldn't you choose to
spend it in Love
rather than in
judgments?

To help children be
free
it would be best
to teach them that
the past
does not have to
predict the future.

May every step
I walk in life
be a prayer of love
and
gratitude.

When you strive to
be
as flexible as
the coconut tree is
in a storm,
you will avoid
all the
backaches of life.

When you are
in
the heart of God,
there is
no getting from here
to there
because
you are already there.

When laughing
becomes
as natural as breathing
we will experience
our
spiritual essence.

We tend to forget
that music
is
one of the best elixirs
for both
emotional and physical
pain.

When love
takes over the universe,
pharmacies
will disappear.

The spring board to
faith and trust
is
to believe in the
sacredness
of
all our children.

To be centered,
focus
on the inner
rather
than the outer.

Silence

is

the music of

heaven

on earth.

Imagination

is

the bridge

to

creativity.

When I truly believe
my thoughts
create my reality,
then
I will choose to have
only
loving thoughts.

Generosity

is

*giving everything from
the heart
with no expectations
of
anything in return.*

Trust that
"change"
may
have positive
rather than negative
results.

Concentrating
only
on the outcome
can
become our
downfall.

*See all your
relationships
as sacred,
and they will mirror
your soul.*

*The sunrise and the
sunset
may be illusions
because
the sun is always
shining
in my heart.*

*If you
want to be happy,
find
a new way
to say
"I love you"
every day.*

True love is never
static
because it is always
expanding
and growing.

There is no such thing
as a "sort of" committed
loving relationship
because
you are either
totally committed
or you are not.

*Marriages that are
half dead
and
filled with judgments,
blame, and guilt
can become fully alive
through
forgiveness.*

*When we put our
total trust
in God,
we don't need an
insurance policy
guaranteeing
our security about
the future.*

*Identify
with a small child's
curiosity
about the world
and
you will never know
boredom.*

Tunnel vision in life
disappears
when we let go
of our belief
in
fear.

The deepest of
friendships
have no expectations
but
are always there
for each other
no matter what.

Whoever invented
fences and boundaries
that separate us
from each other
must have come from
fear because
love knows no
boundaries.

In my life
I want to fly like an
eagle, walk with the
grace of a deer,
and be as friendly as
a puppy dog
always wagging it's
tail with joy.

If we choose to

imagine

everyone

as our Siamese twin,

we

would never hurt

anyone.

If we could only see
the invisible tattoo
that
each of us wears
saying
"I am love."

*May I
resist the temptation
to go
through
life
in a hurry.*

*The fuel
for creative energy
is gratitude.*

*Hearing
is not enough
for
it is listening
that
we must aspire to.*

Perhaps
we focus too much on
the vision of the eyes
rather
than on our
spiritual vision.

*Is it
not better to remember
the love
in our lives,
rather
than the pain?*

*It
is difficult to be
humble
when your ego
wants you
to be special.*

The course of our
lives is determined on
whether we make
decisions based on
love
rather than
fear.

*Perhaps our most
challenging relationship
in life
is to make friends
with ourselves.*

A sense of humor
will
keep you far healthier
than
an apple a day.

To believe in something
that
is greater than ourselves
is
the key
to experiencing
awe.

Rather than worrying
about
what is behind you or
in front of you,
it may be better
to become familiar
with
what is inside you.

*There is really
nothing
to stop you
from
being kind
all
the time.*

*There are times
that
closing your eyes
is
a higher way
of
seeing.*

"To be"
may
be
more important
than
"to do."

*Don't show
your buttons
and
you will find
no one
will
push them.*

*It is not
what is put on our
plate
that is important,
but
how we handle it
that counts.*

Simplicity is difficult
for
a confused mind
to
understand.

When
we are stuck
in our heads,
it is music
that sets
us free.

Love
is listening
and listening
is
Love.

The five senses come
and go,
but the spiritual sense
stays with us
forever.

If like puppy dogs
we would wag our
tails
when happy,
we would never
have backaches.

Find someone
whose only goal in life
is money
and
you will find someone
who feels empty
inside.

Comparisons

give

us

cancer

of

the

soul.

Another secret
that our ego keeps
from us
is that peace of mind
comes from
self-acceptance
and not from seeking
approval from others.

*To love
one another
is
not enough
for
we must love
ourselves
also.*

*To find peace
resist the temptation
to gossip
and
spread rumors.*

Perhaps the biggest
gift humankind
has been given is
the choice
to decide what
thoughts and attitudes
we put in our minds.

*Peace is
when you know that
God
is holding your hand
every step
of the way.*

Open your heart
to God's love
and any need
you have
will disappear.

The desire to serve
others
is
the road to being
ego-less.

Someone would make
a fortune if
they would invent
a garbage disposal
for
the negative thoughts
in our minds.

Dyslexics are smarter
than
most people
because
they know that
dog
and God
are the same.

If
we would make our
heart
the lens
of all that we see,
the world
would be transformed
into love.

Many of us
at some level
do not really believe
that we deserve the
right
to be happy.

*I am
never too old
to make a
difference.*

*My parents taught me
that the best things in
life are free,
and
it took me most
of my life
to prove to myself
that they were right.*

Simplicity

in

a cluttered life

is

like fresh air

in

a stuffy room.

Reverence for life
may
be more important
than
understanding it.

Epilogue

The Wings of Love

May your mind and heart be filled
Only with thoughts of Love

May thoughts of love and forgiveness
Be your way of life

May you be the Light
That shines away the darkness of
Pain, suffering, rejection, and loneliness

May you listen only to the Voice of Love,
The Voice of that which Created you,
To tell you what to think, say, and do

May you continue to remind yourself
By the thoughts that you choose that
We are always connected with God, each other,
And all that is Love

May you continue to know
That happiness, peace,
And joy are your natural state

May you continue to fly
On the Wings of Love
And the Bliss of God,
All the time giving
Thanks for all of your blessings

**Other books by Gerald G. Jampolsky, M.D.
& Diane V. Cirincione, Ph.D.**

*Love is the Answer:
Creating Positive Relationships*

•

*Change Your Mind, Change Your Life:
Concepts in Attitudinal Healing*

•

*Me First and the Gimme Gimmes: A Story of Love
and Forgiveness, Choices and Changes*

•

Wake-Up Calls

Other books by Gerald G. Jampolsky, M.D.

Love Is Letting Go of Fear

•

*To Give Is to Receive: An Eighteen Day Mini-Course
on Healing Relationships*

•

*Teach Only Love: The Twelve Principles
of Attitudinal Healing*

•

*Good-bye to Guilt:
Releasing Fear Through Forgiveness*

(continued)

Out of Darkness into Light:
A Journey of Inner Healing

•

One Person Can Make a Difference:
Ordinary People Doing Extraordinary Things

•

Forgiveness:
The Greatest Healer of All

•

Shortcuts to God:
Finding Peace Quickly Through Practical Spirituality

Other books by Diane V. Cirincione, Ph.D.

Sounds of the Morning Sun

Books by Gerald G. Jampolsky, M.D.
& Lee L. Jampolsky, Ph.D.

Listen to Me: A Book for Men and Women About
Father-Son Relationships

Audiocassettes

Forgiveness:
The Greatest Healer of All

•

Shortcuts to God:
Finding Peace Quickly Through Practical Spirituality

•

Love Is Letting Go of Fear

•

Teach Only Love

•

Good-Bye to Guilt

•

To Give Is to Receive

•

Love Is the Answer:
Creating Positive Relationships

•

Introduction to
A Course in Miracles

•

One Person Can Make a Difference

(continued)

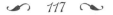

Wake-up Calls

•

The Quiet Mind

•

Achieving Inner Peace

•

Visions of the Future

•

*Finding the Miracle of Love
in Your Life: Based on A Course in Miracles*

Videocassettes

Achieving Inner and Outer Success

•

Healing Relationships

•

Visions of the Future

•

Another Way of Looking at the World

For information about the Center for Attitudinal Healing in Sausalito, California, and its workshops; about other Centers around the world; or about the lectures and workshops of Jerry Jampolsky and Diane Cirincione, please contact

THE CENTER FOR ATTITUDINAL HEALING
33 Buchanon Drive, Sausalito, CA 94965
Phone: (415) 331-6161; Fax: (415) 331-4545
website: **www.healingcenter.org**
email: **home123@aol.com**

If you wish to purchase books and audio- or videotapes, please contact
Miracle Distribution Center
1141 East Ash Ave., Fullerton, CA 92631
Phone: (800) 359-2246
Or contact
The Center for Attitudinal Healing
Sausalito, California

THE FORGIVENESS PROJECT

Welcome to THE FORGIVENESS PROJECT founded by Jerry Jampolsky, M.D. and Diane Cirincione, Ph.D. This ongoing project has many facets, one of which is the collection of fabulous forgiveness stories which may be included in a book.

If you have a story, or know someone else's and would like to submit it, the story should be 1 to 3 pages in length or 150 to 750 words. If a story is selected, your name will be identified with the story.

Please send your stories to us by one of the following means:

E-mail: forgivenessstory@aol.com
Fax: (415) 435-1643
Mail: c/o Jampolsky and Cirincione
　　　 98 Main St. #777
　　　 Tiburon, CA 94920

Thanks for your consideration and don't forget to include your name, address, phone number and e-mail information.

Boundless love,

Jerry and Diane